CONTENTS

Dear Reader

Think of materials and what comes to mind? Bubbling test tubes and evil-smelling potions? Sinister laboratories with scientists in white coats mumbling long complicated chemical names...?

WRONG!

Think of custard!

Custard is a material – that's to say a substance containing chemicals, and a rather interesting one. It's a substance in which droplets of fat float around in liquid. And if you don't believe me why not check your school dinner with a microscope?

yuck!

And custard is just one of thousands of materials that you might come across every day. Really useful, wonderful substances as different as silver and soap or tin and toffee. So for more fascinating facts (not to mention a rather scary story about materials-minded aliens) why not read on? It's more fun than an eyeful of custard!!!

INTRODUCTION

Material Matters has been written especially for you. It contains many of the key facts that you need to know about the fascinating world of materials. Everything in the known universe (including you, custard and alien spacecraft) is made of materials. And materials can be heated and cooled, mixed together and separated. Sometimes these changes can be reversed and sometimes they can't.

So, just file the information in this book between your ears and you'll glide effortlessly through all those school tests without even trying...

edible materials

life-form made
of materials

out-of-this-world materials

SORTING SUBSTANCES

You come across hundreds of different materials in everyday life – everything from custard to concrete. So, how can you tell different materials apart?

The difference is that elephants don't get stuck in custard.

All materials, from wood and plastic to chocolate and flour, have their own properties, such as smell, hardness and colour. Here are some properties to look out for in things at home, at school or in the garden.

NATURAL OR MAN—MADE?

Some natural materials, such as clay, oil and rock, are found underground. Other natural materials come from living things, like wool, wood and cotton. And some substances are made of man-made materials, such as plastic.

from sheep to wool...   clay to mug...   and plastic to bucket

TEXTURE

Touch or soak a substance. Your fingertips can tell the difference between a pile of grit and soft, squashy peat. If you add a little water to peat it will appear to soak it up, but grit doesn't do this.

STRENGTH

Is a substance soft and squishy or hard and stiff? Can you break it without doing yourself an injury?

BENDING AND STRETCHING

Is a substance easy to bend and stretch? You might have difficulty bending an iron bar, but a chocolate bar with a chewy centre is easy-peasy.

hard

easy

The iron bar is hard to stretch, but you can pull the chocolate bar into a longer shape before it comes apart.

ELASTICITY

Some substances (like the iron bar and the chocolate bar) lose their original shape when stretched. Others, like a rubber band, snap back to their original shape. These types of substance are called elastic.

boy about to fire a rubber band

Ouch!

APPEARANCE

Is a material transparent – can light shine through it? Try holding a thin slice of a material up to the light to test it out. Transparent substances include glass and polythene.

CONDUCTIVITY

Will electricity pass through a substance? Electricity flows through metals and people, but not through other materials, such as rubber and plastics.

MAGNETISM

Test whether a substance is magnetic. You can pick up some metals with a magnet, but stone, wood and, once again, rubber and plastics aren't attracted to magnets.

WARNING
Never sniff substances that you don't know. They may be dangerous!

SMELL

You can recognize some substances by their smell. (No, this book won't ask you to rub your nose in fresh squashy cow pats to recognize their smell!)

HEATED MOMENTS

Some materials allow heat to pass through them easily. Scientists say that these substances, including metals, pottery and china, are good conductors of heat. This means that they heat up quickly when left in a warm place.

The heat of the soup travels to the spoon. Metals heat up quickly.

air in gap

Heat can't escape easily – and neither can this fly.

Air isn't a good conductor and that's why the gap inside this double glazing keeps the heat in the room. Air and substances that heat up slowly, such as wood and plastics, are good insulators. That means they do not let heat pass through them easily.

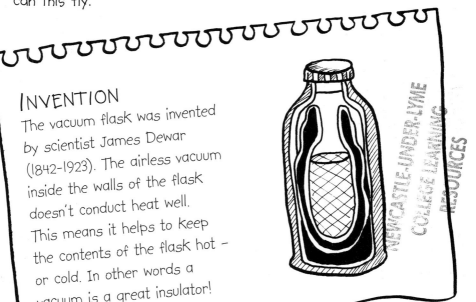

INVENTION

The vacuum flask was invented by scientist James Dewar (1842-1923). The airless vacuum inside the walls of the flask doesn't conduct heat well. This means it helps to keep the contents of the flask hot – or cold. In other words a vacuum is a great insulator!

MAKING CHANGES

my lolly has melted

one hour later...

Heating changes substances. Sometimes the changes can be reversed quite easily. If the sun melts your ice lolly you can catch the liquid in a container and put it in the freezer to make a new lolly.

So what makes it easy? Well, the chemicals that make up the lolly are *still there*. All that's happened is that heat has caused the water in the lolly to change state from water to ice – and if you're in a state wondering what this means take a peek at page 11.

before cooking

But some changes aren't so easy to reverse. Let's check out this rather hearty breakfast...

after cooking

Heating has changed the arrangement of chemicals in the cooked substances – and these chemical changes can't be reversed. Yes, once breakfast is made, it can't be unmade.

BELIEVE IT OR NOT!

Measuring body heat.

You might be gobsmacked to know that at this second *millions* of chemical changes are going on inside your body and they all need heat to work. The measure of heat is temperature and this can be monitored using a thermometer.

GETTING IN A STATE

Any substance on Earth must be in one of three states. It can be a gas – like the atoms in air. It can be solid like a brick, or it can be a liquid like your favourite drink.

The molecules in a gas have lots of space to float around.

The molecules in a solid are packed together and can't move. That's what makes the brick hard.

The molecules in a liquid have some space to slosh around.

Every substance changes at a particular temperature. With me so far?

TAKE WATER AS AN EXAMPLE...

Water freezes into a solid at 0°C. We call this solid ice. Above 0°C water is just plain boring old water – a liquid. Like any other liquid, water is runny. When water evaporates it turns into water vapour. Steam from boiling water is actually very hot water vapour. Like any other gas the vapour floats away in the air. The brilliant thing is that these changes can be reversed just by altering the temperature.

ice

water

water vapour

BELIEVE IT OR NOT!

Water also becomes vapour when it evaporates from the sea.
The vapour rises and cools into droplets (that's what clouds are).
This process is called condensation. As they cool further the
droplets get bigger and fall as rain. Who says science is wet?

THE WATER CYCLE

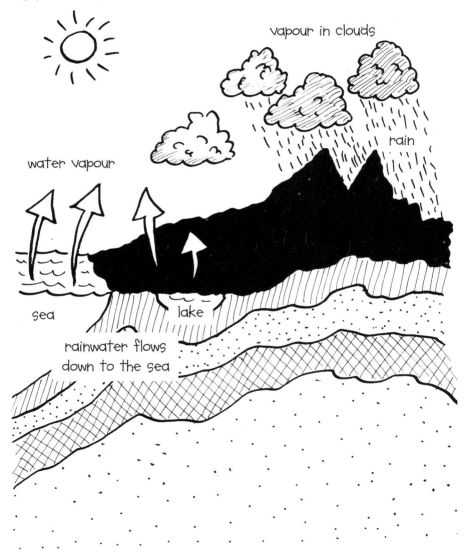

vapour in clouds

rain

water vapour

sea   lake

rainwater flows
down to the sea

WONDERFUL WATER

Water has loads of incredible properties...
It has a 'skin' made of molecules pulling
towards each other. The skin is strong
enough to support a pin, and some
bugs can walk on it without sinking.

When water freezes it expands – that's because the ice pushes
out as it forms. This is bad because expanding ice bursts pipes
and crushes ships. But because ice takes up more space than
water, it's lighter for its size (scientists say it's less dense) than
water. As a result, ice floats on water, fish don't get frozen into
ponds and penguins have somewhere to live.

Lots of substances dissolve in water.
Take salt for example. Imagine
adding it to your dad's tea (beware
you could get a-salted for this).

Tea is made mainly of hot
water. Salt dissolves in tea.

Salty taste proves salt
chemicals are still there.

Now read on for more dissolving facts...

13

MIXING AND SEPARATING

Suppose you mix two substances by mistake – well don't worry. As long as there aren't chemical changes that can't be reversed – you can un-mix them with a few scientific tricks.

The larger grains of sand are caught in the sieve.

Imagine you're having a picnic on a beach and sand gets in the sugar. You could separate the larger grains of sand with a sieve.

Now add warm water to the mixture that came through the sieve. Like the salt on page 13, sugar dissolves in water but sand doesn't! Much of the sand will sink to the bottom of the sieve and you can pour off the liquid or decant it as a scientist would say.

Next filter the liquid through a coffee filter into a bowl. Tiny bits of sand will be caught, leaving only the sugary water.

Leave the water to evaporate in the sun and you'll be left with the sugar to put in your mum's tea! Got all that? Well, now you can relax... it's story time!

The aliens next door

Mike knew there was something odd about the neighbours. And that was before Mr Moebius ate a struggling fly and announced that he came from the planet Xenon.

It all began one morning when Mike and his parents were eating breakfast.

'Saw Mr Moebius,' Mike's dad was saying between mouthfuls. 'He asked me if Mike could help him with some DIY. He says he'll pay.' Mike felt a cold shiver run down his spine.

'What did you say?' asked Mike's mum, looking up from her paper.

'Well, I said I'd ask Mike,' said his dad.

'I think he's weird!' said Mike darkly.

Mike's mum laughed and ruffled his hair. 'Well, let's hope his money is the right colour.'

'And let's hope you can save it for Christmas!' said Mike's dad. What do they know? Mike thought bitterly as he rang the doorbell. They're supposed to be teachers. They're supposed to care about children instead of packing them off to strange houses.

Myra answered the door. Mike didn't like her – there was something unearthly about the way she looked. She had pale skin and pale blue eyes and very black hair, and she wore black clothes.

'Oh, so you've come,' she said flatly, folding her arms.

'Worse luck!' said Mike grumpily.

Mr Moebius appeared behind his daughter. Mike was surprised by how old he looked with his unsmiling grey face and thinning white hair.

'Follow me,' he ordered.

The house was as clean and unwelcoming as an operating theatre. All the surfaces were white, all the furniture looked unused and the carpets unworn. It was almost as if no one lived there.

16

Mr Moebius handed Mike a bucket saying, 'fill this receptacle with H_2O and decant it into the propulsion molecule compressor.'

'What?' said Mike, feeling stupid.

'It's simple – he means fill the bucket with water and pour it into the tank,' whispered Myra.

Mike went to the kitchen tap and did as he was told, pouring the heavy bucket of water into the funnel of a large shiny tank, its sides covered with a network of small pipes. He did this again and again but the tank showed no sign of filling.

Myra followed him out to the kitchen. 'And try not to spill half of it,' she hissed.

'So, what's in that tank?' asked Mike crossly.

'What's it to you? OK – I'll tell you, there's a chemical in the tank that mixes with the water to make fuel for the craft – got it?'

'So why can't your dad do this job?' Mike asked.

'He's not well, he keeps getting... tired,' said Myra.

Returning to the front room, Mike suddenly froze. He gasped in terror and the bucket fell from his hand, spilling water everywhere. Sitting where Mr Moebius had been was

17

a wriggling mass of grey tentacles! Then he saw Myra looking alarmed and even paler than usual.

'He needs his fungus!' she said urgently. She opened a cupboard and took out a tray of mushrooms. Quickly she chopped up several and took them to the Thing.

Mike heard a munching slurping noise and when he looked again there was Mr Moebius sitting exactly as before and looking as if nothing had happened.

'Chitin,' he whispered. 'It's an essential nutrient. I seem to need more of it since my power cell started failing.' Myra put her hand on her father's shoulder. 'Well dad, you are 750 years old. You should be taking it easy!' And then she remembered Mike was watching.

'You can go now,' she told him coldly.

'What's going on?' asked Mike at the door.

'We're going home,' said Myra curtly, 'back to our planet.' And with that she closed the door.

IT'S A FACT
Chitin (ki-tin) is a tough substance found in mushrooms and other fungi.

18

Mike's family were eating spaghetti on toast.

'What time is it?' asked Mike's dad. He was too busy eating to look at his watch.

'Seven,' said his mum.

'Seven!' he exclaimed. 'You'd better hurry – the meeting's at half past!'

'Mr Moebius is an alien,' said Mike.

'Yes OK, Mike,' sighed his mum.

'He IS an alien!' Mike repeated. 'I saw him change into a monster and eat raw mushrooms.'

'Well, you'd best eat your spaghetti,' she laughed, 'otherwise I might turn into a monster too.'

'Did you know,' said Mike's dad looking serious, 'that spaghetti grows on trees, and it's a real hassle to harvest?'

'Don't listen to him – it's wheat flour and water,' said Mike's mum with a smile. 'It's squeezed through holes to make it thin.'

IT'S A FACT
Adding water forms a substance in flour called gluten into long strands. The gluten strengthens the pasta and the water makes it soft enough to shape.

'Mum, I've got to speak to you,' said Mike, pushing his parents' bedroom door open. Supper was over and Mike's mum was sitting in front of the mirror putting on lipstick.

'Mmmm?' she said.

'It's Mr Moebius – he's an alien!'

'Thought you said he was a mushroom?' said Mike's mum without much enthusiasm.

IT'S A FACT
Lipstick is made from waxes and oils. These substances don't mix with water so they won't wash off when you drink.

Then she turned to the mirror and dabbed her lips.

'Are you ready?' Mike's dad called.

'You don't believe me!' said Mike desperately.

'Of course I do darling!' said Mike's mum hastily, and gave him a lipsticky kiss. 'Sorry,' she said, 'it's only waxes and oils,' and she licked her finger and tried to rub it off.

Two weeks later Myra called for Mike. 'I thought you were coming round. The work isn't finished!' she said sternly.

'Oh yes – do go!' said Mike's mum, and before he could reply she'd propelled him out the door with an absent-minded kiss. She was already thinking of the pile of GCSE projects she had to mark.

Mr Moebius was waiting on his doorstep.

'When did you order the lacquer?' he asked Myra.

'Last week and confirmed by mind-mail,' said Myra.

'And the diamonds for the windows?'

'At the same time.'

'So what's this lacquer stuff?' said Mike who was feeling lost.

Myra steered him to the back window.

'It's protection. When we leave your atmosphere the friction between the air and craft will heat it up – it's like rubbing your hands to make them warm. The lacquer insulates the rest of the craft from the heat. Anyway this is what we've been doing since you last bothered to come round.'

Mike gasped. There before him on the back lawn was a saucer-shaped craft about six metres across. Just large enough to take Myra and her father to the stars.

'I never saw it!' he gasped.

'The cloaking device is operational,' said Mr Moebius with an air of quiet satisfaction.

'The lacquer should dry in no time,' said Myra.

'Yes,' said Mr Moebius. 'Atmospheric conditions indicate rapid evaporation.'

Myra handed Mike a large paintbrush, some goggles and a thick pair of gloves.

'Careful,' she murmured, 'you don't want to get this stuff on your skin or in your eyes. Well don't just stand there – start painting!'

21

The lacquer had no smell and no colour. It looked just like water... maybe it was water. But with Myra's warning still on his mind, Mike decided not to lick a drop from his glove.

'It won't exactly kill you,' said Myra working on the other side of the craft. 'But you might be left with a purple tongue for a few weeks.'

Mike hastily dipped his brush back into the pot. He was sure that he'd heard Myra's voice in his head. Had she ever spoken normally?

'It's confirmed,' said Mr Moebius. 'Mind-mail from Xenon. We go on 5 November local star-date.'

Suddenly his head jerked. 'Look there – a fly!' he cried.

Mike thought he saw the
old man's tongue shoot out
and grab the struggling insect.

'Chitin,' Mr Moebius
mumbled contentedly,
'it's essential'.

Mike was so shocked that he banged a small dent in
the smooth metal of the spacecraft. But as he gazed at
the blemish in horror it rapidly disappeared leaving
a smooth surface again.

'Memory metal,'
said Myra's voice from
inside his head.
'It remembers the
shape it's meant to
be in and repairs itself.'

It was Bonfire
Night. Mike's dad was
rummaging in his coat
pockets for his gloves and peering expectantly at the sky.

'They're going tonight,' said Mike.

'Going? Who's going?' asked his dad.

'I told you, Mr Moebius and Myra are going back to
their own planet tonight.'

'I don't blame them,' said Mike's dad blowing on his hands.
'It's too darn cold here. So when are these fireworks starting?'

'Soon I think,' said Mike's mum. 'Fireworks are
fascinating, Mike. They're gunpowder with stuff like
strontium added for colour.'

Mike sighed. 'You're not teaching now, mum,' he wanted

to say, but instead he said, 'Mr Moebius said people would be watching the fireworks and wouldn't notice the craft.'

'Oh dear, does that mean we'll miss it?' said Mike's mum shepherding him in front of her.

Just then the first rocket went up with a whoosh and a bang and a shower of sparks. The people waiting in the park oohed and aahed at the explosions of colour and light. But Mike was silent. A dreadful thought had just struck him – perhaps it was all a joke! Some complicated plot just to make him look silly! Perhaps Mr Moebius was an ordinary person – a little odd maybe, but a human just like everyone else.

And yet... He was still wondering when there was a terrific BANG! from the direction of the neighbours' house.

Everyone turned to look,
but only Mike saw the dark
saucer flit into the night sky.
'WOW – that was some
banger!' said Mike's dad.
Mike said nothing. In
his head he was saying
goodbye and in his head
he heard Myra say,
'so long, Earthling!'

Mike's hand was
clenched tight in
his coat pocket.
Just then he felt
something hard and
round that hadn't
been there a moment before.
He pulled it out and gazed in
wonder. A small disc gleamed in
the weak light.

'It's gold, stupid,' said
the voice in his head.
Then another voice spoke.
It was Mr Moebius.

'Pure metallic material
made from stars – it's
valuable on your planet,
I believe. Consider it payment.'

IT'S A FACT
All gold was
made by exploding
stars before the
Earth formed.

Mike gazed up at the sky. The spacecraft climbed
faster and faster and higher and higher in a glittering
shower of fireworks until at last it vanished into
the wide, majestic sky.

QUIZ TIME

Now just to make sure that you've been paying attention, here's a little quiz to test your memory.

STORY QUIZ

Some of these statements are true and some are made up.
See if you can guess the correct answers.

1 Water can be used as fuel.

2 Diamonds can be used to make windows.

3 Lacquer can be used to protect spacecraft.

4 Metals that can be dented and yet return to their original shape really exist.

WACKY INVENTIONS

Why are these inventions impossible?

1 A chocolate windowpane (you can eat it when you get hungry).

2 A match you can strike twice.

3 A candle that never melts.

4 Ice-cream that doesn't melt.

5 Reusable coal.

6 A magnet that picks up Wellington boots.

7 Rubber electrical wire.

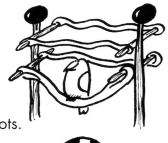

WHAT'S IN A WORD?

What can you do with a buckyball?

a Kick it.

b Eat it.

c Put atoms inside it.

WHAT'S GOING ON?
Why is the mirror wet?

cold mirror

steam (water vapour)

rubber duck

Clue: what happens to water vapour when you cool it down?

WHAT DO THEY HAVE IN COMMON?
Find the connections between the items in each question ...
1 A banana and a polythene bag.
2 Concrete and glass.
3 The chemicals sodium and chlorine.
4 The mercury in a thermometer and a substance called gallium.
5 Fudge and toffee.
6 Ink and tennis rackets.

Connections
a They're made out of sugar.
b They bend in high winds.
c They contain the substance ethylene (eth-y-leen).
d They're found in salt.
e They're types of metal.
f They're made out of carbon.

The answers are on the next page.

QUIZ TIME ANSWERS

STORY QUIZ

1 Water is not used as a fuel although it contains hydrogen which can be used as a fuel.

2 Diamonds can withstand high temperatures, and they have been used for spacecraft windows.

3 The lacquer was made up.

4 Yes, memory metals really do exist! A material called nitinol (ny-tin-nol) can be bent but will return to its original shape.

WACKY INVENTIONS

1 Chocolate doesn't let light through and the hot sun might melt it.

2 When matches are used the chemicals in the head and wood are burnt up. Burning is a change that can't be reversed, so the match can't be struck twice.

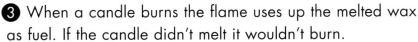

3 When a candle burns the flame uses up the melted wax as fuel. If the candle didn't melt it wouldn't burn.

4 If ice-cream didn't melt in your mouth, it would be very hard and cold and difficult to eat.

5 When coal is burnt it's destroyed. This change cannot be reversed – so the coal can't be used again.

6 Plastics aren't magnetic (see page 8).

7 An electrical current can run through metals, but not through rubber.

What's in a word?

c A buckyball, or buckminsterfullerene (buck-min-ster-full-er-reen), is a tiny ball of a substance called carbon. The ball is hollow inside and ideal to put atoms in. Although buckyballs sound like science fiction they're actually found in common old soot.

What's going on?

Steam forms on the mirror because the heat has turned some bath water to vapour. As the water molecules in the gas touch the cool mirror they cool and form water droplets. This another example of condensation (look back to page 12).

Cool mirror!

What do they have in common?

1c Ethylene gas is made by ripening bananas and causes nearby bananas to ripen too. The ethylene in polythene is made from naphtha (nap-tha), an oil by-product, or natural gas.

pardon!

2b Surprisingly both concrete and glass are slightly elastic (to check what this word means see page 7).

3d Sodium and chlorine are both poisonous, but together they're harmless and vital for health!

4e The other connection is that mercury and gallium are liquid at room temperatures. Gallium actually melts in your hand.

5a They're different because the sugar has been heated to different temperatures.

6f Ink is made from carbon and tennis rackets are made from tough, springy carbon fibre.

SCIENCE SUPERSTARS

The science of materials is all about substances and how they can be changed, for example by heating or by mixing them with other substances. Meet some of the people who uncovered the mysteries of materials and discovered some seriously strange substances.

TO BEGIN AT THE BEGINNING...

Ancient people were fascinated by materials and must have enjoyed heating and mixing them to find out what happens. This lead to the discovery of new materials, such as glass, by the ancient Egyptians around 2500 BC.

People also experimented with metals and in 1500 BC the Hittite people of Turkey found out how to make and fashion iron. By AD 700 craftspeople in China were making the fine pottery known as porcelain.

ANTOINE LAVOISIER
(1743–1794)
Nationality: French
Claim to fame: helped to put chemistry on a scientific basis.

For thousands of years people mixed materials and used trial and error to get a result.
Lavoisier encouraged scientists to weigh chemicals carefully before mixing and to measure their results. This allowed other scientists to repeat the tests. Helped by his wife, Marie, he discovered that burning requires a gas found in air called oxygen. He also proved that water is made up of oxygen and another substance normally found as a gas, hydrogen. But Lavoisier worked as a tax collector and when revolution hit France in 1789 tax collectors became unpopular. The scientist went into hiding, but he was caught and executed.

BELIEVE IT OR NOT!
When Lavoisier was at school he studied nothing but maths for one year followed by two years of philosophy. Fine... if you like that sort of thing!

31

INVENTION

The rubber used in boots and bike tyres has to be treated so that it doesn't become soft or easily breakable. This process, involving heating rubber with a substance called sulphur, was invented by American Charles Goodyear (1800–1860). Goodyear spent his life attempting to discover this treatment and became so poor that he was arrested for not paying his bills. After the discovery others stole his idea and he died a poor man.

MARIE CURIE
(1867–1934)
Otherwise known as:
Manya Sklodowska
Nationality: Polish/French
Claim to fame: discovered two new substances, polonium and radium.

Young Marie (Polish name Manya) had a tough childhood. Her mum and sister died of disease and her dad lost his job as a teacher. At the time Poland was ruled by Russia and children were forced to learn all their lessons at school in the Russian language. Somehow Manya scraped together the money to go to university in Paris. There she was very poor and all she could afford to eat were tea, bread and margarine, but she still managed to pass her exams and get a job in a laboratory. She married her boss, Pierre Curie, and they discovered polonium and radium by pounding and boiling industrial waste in a leaky old shed.

BELIEVE IT OR NOT!
When Marie Curie visited America in 1921 she was given one gram of radium as a present. Radium was so rare and valuable that the gift was worth $100,000!

AND TODAY...
There are chemists in every country. Many work in industry developing new substances that will appear in our clothes and foods and fuels in the future. One of the most exciting new research areas is nanotechnology, which involves building tiny machines atom by atom using chemicals such as buckyballs.

And if you fancy doing a bit of science yourself, you can start by turning this page ...

SECRET SCIENCE EXPERIMENTS

Scientist Vera Fye has kindly allowed us a peek at her experiment notebooks...

Dear Reader
Experiments are vital for scientists to test out scientific ideas and develop new scientific knowledge. It's always a good idea to plan your experiments carefully and think in advance what you want to find out and what you're expecting the experiment to show. Keep accurate records and charts of your results and don't be afraid to repeat a test in order to check what happened.
Good Luck!
Vera Fye

MAKE YOUR OWN BEACH!

So you can't get to the seaside?
Oh well, here's the next best thing!

YOU WILL NEED
★ An old square washing-up bowl
★ Four heaped tablespoonfuls of sand
★ Salt
★ A ruler

1 Fill the bowl with 1 cm of warm water and stir in 4 dessertspoonfuls of salt to make it like seawater.

2 Add the sand and mix well.

3 Wait for the water to clear. This should take about one hour.

4 If you hold the bowl at a slight angle you can make a beach. You can make gentle waves with your hand.

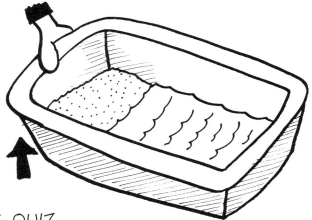

QUICK QUIZ

1 What sinks to the bottom, which floats in the water and what is dissolved in the water so you can't see it?

2 How might you separate out the salt and the sand?

QUICK QUIZ ANSWERS

1. The larger grains of sand sink. Tiny grains float for a while and make the water murky until they also sink. The salt remains dissolved in the water. 2. Pour the mixture through some coffee filter paper to take out the sand. Allow the water to evaporate and the salt will then reappear.

THE AMAZING USELESS SIEVE

Sieves are great for removing solids from a liquid and they're also great for getting peas out of saucepans – why? – because water drains through the little holes ... well, usually but not always!

YOU WILL NEED

★ A sieve
★ Cooking oil
★ A piece of kitchen paper or old cloth

1 Wipe a generous amount of cooking oil all over the sieve, inside and out.

2 What do you think will happen if you drip a few drops of water on to the sieve?

HERE'S WHAT HAPPENS...

Not all the water goes though the sieve. Why is this?

SCIENCE SECRET

Oil is a type of fat and oil and water don't mix. The oil narrows the holes of the sieve and make it harder for the drops of water to get through.

Fizzing with Energy

To do anythIng you need energy. And energy is just as vital for chemical changes – as you're about to discover...

YOU WILL NEED
★ Two vitamin C tablets
★ Two clear bowls
★ A measuring jug filled with 200 ml of water

1 Put the water in the fridge for two hours.
2 Pour the water into one of the bowls.

3 Now fill the jug with 200 ml of water from the hot tap (this water should be as hot as you can make it).

WARNING
Be very careful with hot water from the tap as it can scald.

4 Carefully pour the hot water into the second bowl.

5 Place a vitamin C tablet in each bowl.

Here's What Happens

Both tablets start fizzing as a chemical change takes place. But the tablet in the hot water fizzes faster and dissolves quicker than the tablet in cold water.

Science Secret

Remember how heat is vital for some chemical changes? (Go to page 10 if you don't.) Hot water molecules have more heat energy than cold water molecules and this allows a tablet to dissolve more quickly in hot water.

THE BAFFLING BUBBLING HANKIE

We're not talking snotty noses and colds here – we're talking science. Remember the sieve that didn't sieve? It's also possible for water not to soak through a cloth. Try it if you don't believe me...

YOU WILL NEED
★ A cloth handkerchief (a tea towel or kitchen cloth will do just fine)
★ A glass
★ An elastic band

1 Fill the glass three-quarters full with water.

2 Cover the glass with the cloth and secure it with the elastic band.

3 What do you think will happen if you turn the glass upside down? Do this over the sink please (not your little brother's head).

4 Prod the underside of the cloth with your finger. So what's happening and why?

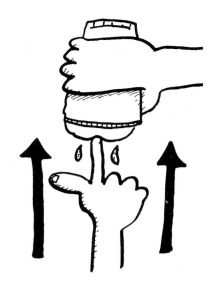

HERE'S WHAT HAPPENS...
So you thought that water soaks through cloth? Not necessarily – a bit does but most doesn't. When you prod the cloth more water drips through and little bubbles start rising in the water.

SCIENCE SECRET
Some materials are absorbent – that's to say they soak up liquids. Examples include the peat on page 7, toilet paper and most cloth. In this case, though, the water is trapped in the glass by the air pushing through the holes in the cloth. By prodding the cloth you force water though the holes in the cloth which makes a gap for air bubbles to force their way through from the outside.

CHEMICAL KALEIDOSCOPE
Bright and cheerful are the words that spring to mind when you make this messy mixture. But make sure you do it on newspaper otherwise your parents will have a few words to say!

YOU WILL NEED
★ Some food colours
★ Milk
★ A saucer or small dinner plate
★ Washing-up liquid
★ A plastic straw

1 Fill the saucer with milk.

2 Use the end of the straw to pick up and then add a drop of each food colour to different places in the milk. (Don't forget to wash the straw after each colour.)

3 What do you think will happen when you add a drop of washing up liquid to the centre of the saucer? Do it and be amazed!

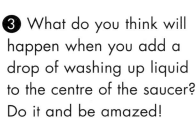

WHAT HAPPENS...
The colours start swirling around and mixing in weird patterns. So what's causing this?

WARNING
Do not do this in the cat's saucer. She might get the shock of her nine lives!

SCIENCE SECRET
Milk is a mixture of water and fat and other things. Washing up liquid contains chemicals that break up the surface of the milk. This sets up currents in the milk that make the food colours swirl around.

CLEARLY BETTER!

Tired of boring old grey ice? Here's your chance to make some lovely shiny deluxe, see through ice, and you can find out the science behind it at the same time!

YOU WILL NEED
★ An ice tray with a few squares free
★ A freezer
★ A kettle

1 Boil some water in the kettle and then allow it to stand for a minute.

2 Pour the hot water into the free squares in the ice tray.

3 Return the tray to the freezer and leave it for two hours.

HERE'S WHAT HAPPENS

Your new ice cubes will be clear and transparent (remember that word?) but the old ice is grey.

SCIENCE SECRETS

The grey colour is made up of trapped air bubbles in the centre of the ice cube. Air dissolved in the water formed the bubbles as it froze. But boiling removes most of this air and because the water is hot it freezes slowly and allows the remaining air to escape. So, in your new cubes there are no bubbles and clear ice!. Well, I'm glad that's cleared up – have an 'ice' day!

THAT'S ASTONISHING!

⭐ BIG BANG

You breathe hydrogen atoms in the air with every breath and drink hydrogen atoms with every glass of water (see page 28). Hydrogen was made in the Big Bang – the huge explosion that started the universe about 15 billion years ago.

⭐ HOLE IN THE GROUND

The substances yttrium, erbium and terbium are named after a quarry at Ytterby in Sweden where they were found in 1843. Later on another newly discovered substance was called ytterbium in honour of this famous hole in the ground.

⭐ SMELLY CHEMICALS

Some substances are very smelly. Garlic, rotten eggs and onions all smell pretty strong, but they have something else in common too. They contain a substance called sulphur. If you eat garlic or onions the chemical gets into your blood and comes out in smelly breath.

★ MOSQUITO KILLER

In 1999 Indian scientists found that disease-carrying mosquitoes are driven away by the smell of peppermint. And peppermint oil actually kills young mosquitoes. So will the treatment work for everyone? I guess you'll have to suck it and see.

★ POTENT PERFUMES

Smells can last thousands of years – and we're not talking about your little brother's trainers or the cat pee behind the sofa. No, when the 3000-year-old tomb of Tutankhamun was found in Egypt in 1922, the smelly perfumes left with the king's body were still whiffy after all these years.

★ PVC POOL

PVC or as a scientist might call it polyvinyl chloride (polly-vi-nul claw-ride) is best known to your parents as the plastic raw material of their prehistoric rock records. But did you know that it was used to line the bottom of a volcano crater on the island of Tenerife? The crater was filled with water to make a reservoir. Wat-er record achievement!

ACCIDENTAL GAS

Some substances were discovered by accident. For example acetylene (a-set-a-leen) gas – the gas burnt in welding torches – was discovered in 1892. Inventor Theobald Wilson was trying to make another chemical, calcium, from lime and iron, but ended up with a revolting black lump. He angrily chucked the lump in the nearest stream and the water started to bubble. The black substance mixed with water to make acetylene gas. Weld done that man!

CHANGING SUBSTANCES

Some substances decay and that's why books can self-destruct. It's sad but true that after about 100 years books containing paper with lots of acid (added acid and natural acids in the wood) become brittle as the fibres are slowly eaten away. Eventually the pages fall apart if they're turned.

★ Ouch, ouch, ouch!

Stinging nettles and ant stings are painful for precisely the same reason. They both contain a substance called formic acid which irritates your skin. You'd be a little rash if you rubbed either of these on your body.

★ Buzz off

Bee stings really hurt because they contain another type of acid. To stop the pain you can use bicarbonate of soda, a substance that stops the acid working.

★ Fancy an omelette?

Ever wondered why eggs go white when you cook them? No, it's not because they're scared of being eaten. All white, I'll tell you – the whites contain molecules called proteins that take the form of tight balls of material. They unravel when heated to make the white colour and this is an irreversible change.

Goodbye...

Well, that's all. As you have seen there's more to chemicals than strange scientists and mixed-up materials. There's an immense range of useful and useless materials and without them the world just wouldn't be the same.

So don't forget, materials matter mightily!

GLOSSARY

ABSORBENT A substance is absorbent if it can soak up liquids such as water easily.

Kitchen paper is a good example of an absorbent material – ideal for those embarrassing little spills!

ATOM The smallest object that makes up a chemical. Most of the atoms on Earth are joined together to make molecules.

CHEMICAL Any substance made or studied by scientists.

CONDENSATION When water vapour is cooled below a certain temperature it turns into droplets of water.

CONDUCTIVITY When heat passes through an object.

CONDUCTOR A substance that allows heat to pass through it.

DENSITY How much matter is packed into an object. People generally measure density by weighing and measuring volume.

DISSOLVE A substance is mixed with liquid and breaks down into molecules.

ELASTIC No, we're not talking about the stuff that holds up knickers! An elastic substance is one that you can stretch and it will return to its original shape.

EVAPORATION
This is what
happens when
a liquid changes
into a gas.

GLUTEN A substance found
in wheat, and in flour made
from wheat.

HITTITES Ancient peoples
from Syria and Asia Minor who
built a great empire around
1400 BC.

INSULATOR
A material that
doesn't allow heat
to pass through it
easily. Insulators
are poor
conductors.

MAGNETIC A chemical that is
attracted to a magnet. Magnetic
substances contain metals such
as iron.

MOLECULE A collection
of atoms joined together.

MONITOR To check or
measure something.

OXYGEN This gas makes up
one fifth of the air we breathe.
It is vital for life.

PEAT The remains of
dead plants that have been
squashed into a swamp. Peat
is sometimes burnt as fuel or
used as fertiliser.

TRANSPARENT
A material that
allows light to
pass through it.

VACUUM An empty
space without any air. The
space between stars and
planets is mostly a vacuum.

WATER
VAPOUR
A type of
gas made
up of water
molecules.

INDEX

ROBERT ROLAND

Belitha Press

First published in Great Britain in 2001 by

Belitha Press
An imprint of Chrysalis Books plc
64 Brewery Road, London N7 9NT

Paperback edition first published in 2002

Copyright © Belitha Press Limited 2001
Text by Robert Roland

Editor: Veronica Ross
Designer: Sarah Goodwin
Illustrator: Woody
Consultant: John Stevenson

ISBN 1 84138 180 2 (hb)
ISBN 1 84138 440 2 (pb)

British Library Cataloguing in Publication Data for this
book is available from the British Library.

Printed by Bath Press, England

10 9 8 7 6 5 4 3 2 1 (hb)
10 9 8 7 6 5 4 3 2 1 (pb)

Some of the more unfamiliar words used in this book
are explained in the glossary on pages 46 and 47.